May you always carry HOPE in your heart! Love, Corky & Linda

CORKY
the Wonderdog

Written by Linda Lundquist

Illustrated by Noelle Rollins

Acknowledgments

To my family: Julie, Erika, Paul, Louise, Kieran, Reeve, Elliot, Parker, Sean and Jeff who continue to open their heart to pets and learn the lessons of life and love that they teach us.

To my beloved editor and friend, MaryJo Connolly, whom I lived with in Duluth opening my heart to the beauty around me and story within me.

Thank you to my many angels that encouraged me with this book in so many ways...Glenda Huston, Barb Hynes-Tomczyk, Joan Phillips, Shannon Poppie, Robin Kabusha, Janet Kautz, Deb Young, Julia Schoborg, Vicki Speidel, Anja Hansen, Susan Mullenix, David Hawkinson, Aspen Rollins and so many more!

To my illustrator Noelle Rollins, who kept me afloat on days I felt like I was drowning with paperwork and computer glitches, and whose Illustrations are the essence of Corky's message of love and hope allowing her spirit to live on forever.

Written by: Linda Lundquist
Illustrated by: Noelle Rollins

ISBN: 978-0-578-88826-2

Copyright © 2021

All rights reserved. No part of this book may be reproduced or transmitted in any form by any means, electronic or mechanical, including photocopying and recording, or by any information storage and retrieval system.

Manufactured in United States of America

Table of Contents

Dedication

This book was made possible by you constantly whispering

in my ear, Corky, to help me tell your story.

PROLOGUE

I AM CORKY TALKING TO YOU FROM THE RAINBOW BRIDGE. IT IS A PLACE WHERE WE ANIMALS RETURN TO WAIT FOR OUR BELOVED HUMANS UNTIL THEY JOIN US WHEN IT IS THEIR TIME. I KNEW I HAD TO TELL MY STORY AND IN ORDER TO DO IT I WOULD HAVE TO WHISPER IN LINDA'S EAR. SHE LISTENED WITH AN OPEN HEART AND MY MEMORIES FOLLOW.

FREE TO GOOD HOME

My first family could not take care of me like they wanted to, so they put an advertisement in the paper. The ad said, "Free to good home" but I knew it did not mean that I wasn't worth anything. It meant a new family would come into my life and I would start a new life adventure.

I was so excited when the doorbell rang, and I saw Linda and Louis that I peed on the floor. OH, NO! I was so embarrassed and worried that they wouldn't want me now. I looked into Linda's eyes and saw such kindness and I knew all was well. My food and bowl, water dish, collar, leash, and crate were collected. I ran to the car and jumped in the back seat. I was put in the crate and when Linda saw how I could barely fit into it, she got into the back seat and petted me lovingly all the way home.

Classifieds

Yellow Lab Dog

FREE
to good home

Julie and Erika's
Lemonade Stand

The backyard was all fenced in with a huge silver maple tree and I knew I was going to love this new adventure!

MEETING MY NEW FAMILY

I was so excited for it was the moment I was going to meet my new children. They were at their Dad's house, so Linda decided to walk the two miles with me. She had called to say she was coming with a surprise- which was ME!!!!! The walk was crazy for I had never been walked with a leash and collar. Can you imagine an unsuspecting human being pulled by a canine of eighty-four pounds of solid muscle?

I feel very bad about this, but I pulled and pulled for I didn't like being on a leash with a tight collar. Linda's hand was injured from my pulling as she tried to "rein me in".

Somehow, we got there, and she became aware how I had never been walked before, even though I was now 18 months old. I wondered how old my new kids were, and suddenly the door flew wide open.

Out came two little blond girls bounding down the steps and another still behind the door. Their brother, Paul, wasn't home.

They were so excited to see me I nearly knocked them over with my strength. Their names were Julie and Erika, and they are identical twins who were seven years old. Zoey is their younger sister, but she stayed in the house saying I was too big and jumpy. I licked their faces and knew that I was blessed to have such a wonderful new family.

We headed home and somehow, I managed not to pull so hard. We made it to my new home, and I was given a brown chair just for me. I slept well that first night and fell asleep with a smile on my face.

YES, dogs do smile!

OBEDIENCE TRAINING

When I reflect on this unhappy episode, I understand that sometimes humans, with the best intention, make decisions for pets and children that can sometimes cause unhappiness. Linda, being a Special Education teacher, understood that I needed some kind of training for walking. My rambunctious behavior was not ok when I tried to go on walks with Linda and Louis. They found a training class at a local community center where Julie and Erika could watch the class. The minute I got in there I sensed this was not the place for me. Many of the dogs stared at me with angry looks. The instructor told the owners to line us up in a row and I tried to be brave. The dog next to me gave me a very fierce look. I had never met another dog in my life. I growled from sheer fright. All of a sudden, the instructor came over and picked me up by my leash and collar. She then threw me to the ground. It hurt, and I was so scared and shocked. I looked at Julie and Erika with tears running down their cheeks. Linda was so upset. She wasn't sure what to do. The man next to her whispered, "I know that this is hard to go through for my dog growled and the same thing happened to him." I tried my hardest the rest of the class. It was finally over. As we walked out, Linda said we would never be coming back here again. She believed that harshness with animals and people is not the best way for them to learn. It was the end of obedience school for me. I was thrilled with that decision. I knew that I had to try harder, while still protecting my family, but with no growling at other dogs.

AM I REALLY A LAB?

I was diligently walked almost every day, and my favorite walk was along the Minnehaha Creek and Lake Nokomis. I loved being able to go into the water and cool off on hot summer days.

But there was something that my family could not understand about me. How could I be a Labrador Retriever and be afraid of ducks? Yes, it is assumed that I would be a good breed for retrieving ducks. Not me! Could I be an exception? At first my family made fun of me, and then they realized that I really was afraid of ducks. In the end we all knew, including me, that it was the way I was born. They still loved me for being me. I had taught my two-leggeds about accepting everyone as they are! I was happy inside with that accomplishment.

FAMILY TIMES

The first five years with my new family was the time to get to really know them. I didn't see much of Paul for he was a teenager and spent more time at his Dad's house. He would go on walks with his Mom at times and they would take me to the lake to swim. They would laugh loudly when I would come out of the water and shake myself all over them.

Erika started to teach me a "trick" that made everyone laugh with delight, including her grandparents. I had really long legs and she taught me to back up into a chair sitting on top of the person behind me. I would then stretch my front legs out and felt very comfortable.

Unfortunately, sometimes I stepped on the person's toes who was sitting in the chair. It made everyone laugh, and I knew how important laughter was for my humans. Julie and Erika loved snuggling with me, and I would jump into the bottom bunk for a long time with them. Sometimes they even sneaked me into the bunk to sleep with them.

There was a beautiful red tabby cat named Gingin whom I got to know right away. We got along well, but he sneaked out the door one winter day. My family tried for days to find him. They put signs up everywhere in the neighborhood. A few days later they got a call. It was a very sad time when they found out that he had been hit by a car. That made me feel very sad and I missed him. Two weeks later Linda went down to a sale for Valentine's Day where you can meet kittens and cats to possibly buy. She was just going to LOOK, but of course, she came home with a beautiful gray calico kitten. The girls named her Kiah. She didn't pay much attention to me, but soon another little kitty came into our home. He was named Makade which means black in the Ojibwe language. Mak had gone through a tornado at the horse farm where Linda's sister Robin lived. The kittens were barely six weeks old when the barn was destroyed by the storm, and the mother cat was missing. The kittens had to be given away at that time, for Robin had newborn puppies in the house. Linda was so excited to see the kittens. They had been born on the birthday that Linda and her son shared. She had always wanted a black cat. He came home to live with us which was now two cats and one dog. Mak was very frightened when he came to live with us. We all loved him. OK....I wasn't the nicest dog when he kept cuddling up to me like I was his mother. Our friendship did grow into a deep love. I got used to him needing some loving support from me. Yes, cats and dogs can become great friends and NOT fight. That was another lesson that I came to teach.

One lesson that was painful for me concerned Julie and food-especially candy. I loved that smell the best of all! Julie and Erika had come home from Halloween, (I had no idea what that was except for crazy costumes). They had put their pillowcases on their beds and went to take their showers. I could smell the candy and opened Julie's pillowcase. I couldn't help myself and I started eating and eating the candy. Julie came into the bedroom and let out a piercing scream. I knew that I was in trouble now! Did this precede the biggest lesson I came to teach my family? Possibly, after eating all of the chocolate which is harmful to dogs. Julie learned to forgive me for eating her treats and I learned not to steal my people's food.

Another lesson that I taught, was the day Linda learned why I smelled so good-like cherry almond bark. Erika and Julie had opened one of their mother's hair conditioning bottles and decided to put some on my fur. It turned out that this product was very expensive, and Linda was not happy. I smelled soooo good! OK-time to just smell like a dog from now on. We all laughed about this a little later and I was never "conditioned" again!

LOST AND ALMOST NOT FOUND

I did observe through my years living with my family that they gave everyone a nickname. I learned it was out of love for whomever received the name. Some of my names were Corky Dorky, Bindi, Boo, and others. Some were so strange I just ignored them. What??? This one was the craziest....Corky Dorky Chewy Klutz! I was an athletic dog who was superior at catching balls at the park. Luckily, most of the time my name was just Corky. One day it was shouted for hours. Then I knew I was in trouble.

Linda and her friend Nancy had decided to take me on a long walk in the country. Could I run free like I've always wanted to do? We drove a long way out and the scenery was beautiful. I was a lucky dog to live near a creek and lake, but I had never seen open fields since I came to this family. We stopped and walked over to the Loose Line Trail. I started pulling on my leash. Linda tried to adjust my collar, but I pulled on it. I was FREE...running on the Loose Line Trail.

My long legs bounded forth and I started to run like I was in a marathon. I saw so many new trails to explore. From the top of a hill I heard Linda calling for me. I knew she would find me, so I kept going. What I did not know was that I was running farther from the original trail. Now I was on a country road that was dirt and stones.

I kept running and saw the many birds above me. I started to chase a squirrel into the woods, and I was having quite a fun adventure! I had run a long way from Linda and her friend who were calling my name frantically. I could not hear them and decided to go back. The paths in the woods all looked the same. I was getting thirsty, so I began to look for a creek or a stream. I saw some water, so I ran over to it. Oh, no! I got caught in tons of mud trying to get a drink. Now I looked like a yellow and chocolate lab. Would Linda recognize me?

It had been sometime since I started this adventure. The sun was now in a different place in the sky. I started back to the path I thought was the one to find Linda. It was not the right one. I did not hear anyone calling my name anymore. My super-efficient lab nose that is used to find lost people didn't seem to help me now. I realized I was feeling very hungry and scared. Adventures are great, but I was ready to be done now. I cut through the woods and came out by another road with no cars on it. I crossed the road to a new dirt road that went up to a farmhouse. HMMM...

I smelled some food in the air, and I saw a huge garbage can. I had my nose in the bin quickly. Then I saw Linda and her friend racing up the path. They were screaming my name and Linda ran crying to me. She told me how much she loved me, and we were both overjoyed to see each other. But once I was in the car the tone changed. Linda and her friend were angry at me for running away. I had been on my adventure for over two hours! Linda told me later she would not have given up finding me for she could not tell her children that I was lost. I learned that day that adventures can be great fun, but not when they cause someone else great pain. I promised myself I would never run away again, and I NEVER did!

A TALE ABOUT MY TAIL

A couple months later I ended up with an experience that I was not prepared for. I had gone down the basement when no one was home to look for one of my toys. I backed into something sharp on the wall. OUCH!!! My tail started to hurt. I went upstairs into the kitchen and I had no idea I was getting blood all over the white kitchen cupboards. All of a sudden the back door opened, and Linda and the kids came through the door. Paul shouted, "There is blood all over the kitchen cabinets!" I was standing in the dining room and Erika came over to me shouting that my tail was bloody. Off to the vet we all went. Thankfully I just needed to have it wrapped. I was prescribed antibiotics so I would not get an infection. The trouble is the next day it started to itch and itch. Before I knew it, I had bitten off the bandage the vet had given me.

This time Louis decided to wrap me with electrical tape. It was much harder to do but I managed to get the electrical tape off too. Everyone was getting more frustrated and worried about my healing. Off to the vet for another appointment. This time the vet put this stupid plastic lampshade on my head so I would not chew my tail.

I was Houdini, the famous escape artist, disguised as a lab. I managed to get the lamp-shade off too! My tail was not healing and off to another trip to guess where? Of course, the vet! Dr. Deb suggested another solution, for it was now two months this had been going on. My tail could be docked which would heal much faster. Docked...what did that mean? Were they turning me over on a boat to live the rest of my life? No, it meant that a section of my tail would be cut off a few inches beyond the infection. This time I knew that I must heal, and a lampshade was needed again. I had to try my hardest to quit chewing it off, which helped me heal quickly. Linda used to call my long strong lab tail the "whipper whapper." Now Louis started calling my tail, "the stompy". The whole family soon started calling it by that name. Perhaps it was for the best, for I learned to stop chewing things intended to make me well. We all calmed down and I healed quickly. I was good as new....or so I thought.

BLOOD IN THE SNOW

Our lives were filled with many good things for many years. I got my daily walk and looked forward to weekends when no one was at school or teaching. I was happy that it was a Saturday, for it meant all my family would be home. I had just been let outside to pee. Suddenly I felt so ill I could barely stand up. I heard Julie scream, "Corky is peeing blood in the snow." Somehow, I managed to make it back inside the house. Once inside I started to vomit and shake. Linda called the vet immediately. The vet said to come right away for it was almost time for the clinic to close. It was an awful car ride for I felt so sick. When I looked at my scared family, I felt even worse. I was so sick. I wanted to see the vet and feel better. My family got me to the vet clinic, I had an x-ray, and blood drawn. That hurt a bit, but I knew they needed the blood for information on why I was so sick. I knew I had to be the strong one no matter the outcome. The vet came back into the room, the look on her face was deep concern. My family was told that I had cancer in my kidney. Surgery was needed immediately. I knew this was going to be ok for I knew dogs and humans have two kidneys. My family had to drive me twenty-five miles to another clinic, because my regular vet could not do the surgery. Julie and Erika were so kind, hugging me and telling me how much they loved me on the way down to the surgery. I could not bear the fact that this could be my last day on Earth. My purpose this lifetime was about HOPE in the darkest hours. I knew that I MUST survive this surgery and get well. They brought out a gurney for me that was human size for I was such a large dog and couldn't walk now. The vets and assistants were very kind. My family kissed me good-bye with tears in their eyes. They wheeled me to surgery immediately. The bright lights above me faded from view as they gave me an anesthesia to sleep during the surgery. I sent love to my family as the room twirled in my brain and I fell asleep.

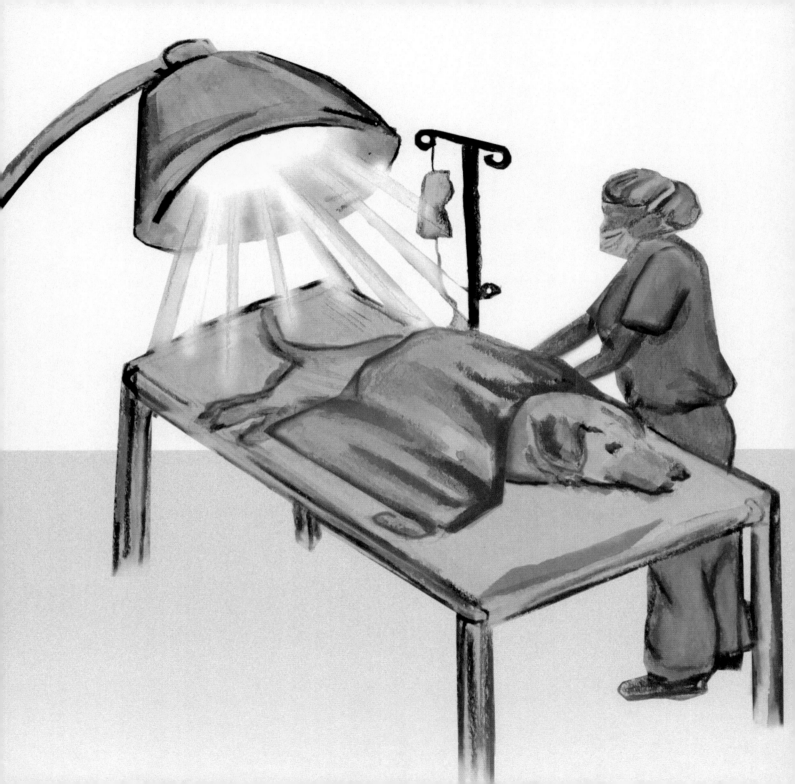

THE MORNING AFTER

I woke up a few hours after my surgery, feeling groggy and sore. I knew I was going to be OK! The vets all took such kind and loving care of me. The next morning my family was called to come and get me in the afternoon. When they arrived, I could see big smiles on their faces as they approached me.

I wanted to jump for joy, but I had to listen and walk slowly. I did not want to tear my stitches open. The vet talked to Linda for a few moments in the corner of the room. I did not know that Linda was told that the cancer was very aggressive. I had only a few months to live. They were to keep me comfortable and love me up as much as possible. No one knew exactly how much time I had left. I knew the truth that there was a better outcome. I saw the sadness in Linda and Louis' eyes. The children did not know the whole truth at that time until awhile later. I was determined to live my purpose of teaching HOPE and it started NOW!

THE MEDICINE POUCH

Linda was teaching at a school where the majority of the children were American Indian. She tried to be cheerful at school but the children sensed that something was bothering her. They listened as she told them about me. Suddenly they were all saying that I needed a medicine pouch. Linda was not sure what that was. The children explained that it is a pouch, usually made from deer skin, that many times is worn around the neck. It is filled with items such as herbs and precious stones, to help with healing or protection.

She went to the store where they said to buy me a pouch. I loved it when she put it around my neck so I could smell the healing herbs. Wearing this pouch made me feel important and loved. At the same time my family bought me a new navy-blue chair to make it easier for me after my surgery. The lesson of HOPE began! I started to feel better almost immediately. Soon my appetite came back and I could go outside on walks. Days spilled into months and then years.

I was still alive. One day I knew that I needed to teach my family one of the most important lessons of all. I was alone in the kitchen with Linda. She smiled at me. I sat down and chewed off the medicine pouch. I had worn it for almost three and a half years. I knew that I was totally healed. I didn't need the pouch anymore! Off it went onto the kitchen floor. Linda gasped for a moment. I looked deeply into her eyes. I said to her, "I am healed, and it is time to say good-bye to what helped me. You humans hang onto so many things that you don't need anymore because of fear. YOU MUST LEARN TO LET GO AND TRUST. Trust that all will be well. You must have faith and deep hope whatever the outcome." Linda hugged me and from then on I knew my purpose had been understood. Deep HOPE must be present no matter what is happening around you. There will be times things don't turn out the way you want them to, but that is another lesson for another time.

MY LAST ADVENTURE

I was seven when the cancerous kidney was removed. Now I was...are you ready for it...sixteen! The many years that followed my surgery were very happy. Eventually as I aged, I started to slow down. I still went for shorter walks and I was always loved deeply by my family. I had developed a lump on my leg, when the vet examined it she said that it was cancer. My family needed to watch when it grew larger. I would need another exam with the vet when that happened. Linda monitored me every day for several months. I started to feel very tired and not as hungry now. The lump started to increase in size so I went back to the vet. Unfortunately, I was too old to have surgery. Since I was not feeling well at all, we all knew that it was soon to be my time to leave this life. Although everyone showered me with hugs and kisses, I was aware of the sad looks on their faces. The day came for Linda to call the vet, and she said that the lump had grown much larger the past several days. The vet told her I would be in pain soon, so we chose to call a traveling vet to come to our house in two days for our good-byes.

The next day Linda decided to go up to Lake Superior which has always been one of her favorite places to visit. As she was going out the door she looked at me. I begged with my eyes for her to take me along for the ride. I was ready for one last adventure. I sat up and stared right at her and she could not believe how perky I became. I jumped down off my chair and wagged my tail. The next minute Linda was crying and hugging me. She decided to take me

Along and got extra blankets so I would be comfortable riding in the car. I walked slowly out to the car for the last time. I wanted to be with her, and I slept most of the two and a half hours to get up there.

When I woke up and saw the huge lake, I felt a surge of energy shoot through my tired body. I jumped out and started to walk on the rocks at Brighton Beach Park/Gitchi-Gammi. The Objibwe throughout time have called Lake Superior Gitchi-Gammi (with many different spellings). We walked slowly and sat at the gazebo overlooking the lake. My last adventure was going to another beach called Burlington Bay. I got to see one of the big ships on Lake Superior that travel around the world. I could barely walk back to the car by the end of the trip. Linda helped me in and I slept soundly the whole way home.

SAYING GOOD-BYES

Two days later there was a stillness and sadness that I could feel when I woke up. The traveling vet was coming to our house so my family could be with me in the place I had loved. It was Solstice, June 21st, and a beautiful warm sunny day. The vet said he would be over in a few hours. I would probably need some medicine for me to be totally relaxed. What? I was calm and knew it was time to say good-bye to my beloved family. I had taught them so many things. I felt like I had lived my life purposes.

They were all by my side for hours telling me how much they loved me. Neighbors came by and petted me one last time with tears in their eyes. Soon there was a knock at the door, and it was the vet. He had such a kind gentleness about him that I knew all would be well. I didn't need anything to calm me down. I wanted one more sniff of the beautiful summer day. I got up and went to the screen door. I imagined I was outside smelling flowers, feeling the wind blow, and saw children playing outside. I felt such happiness and joy. I had lived NINE years longer than anyone would have thought after being so sick. I had taught about HOPE and LOVE. It was a perfect day to end this life adventure. Perhaps I would be back starting another one very soon, who knows?

THE END (but not really!)

EPILOGUE

MANY YEARS HAVE PASSED SINCE I CROSSED OVER TO THE RAINBOW BRIDGE.

DURING THOSE YEARS LINDA WAS BLESSED WITH TWO WONDERFUL GRANDSONS WHOSE NAMES ARE KIERAN AND REEVE. THEY ARE VERY CLOSE TO THEIR GRAMMY AND SHE HAS AMUSED THEM WITH STORIES ABOUT ME.

WOULDN'T YOU KNOW THAT THESE BOYS ALSO HAD A LAB/GOLDEN RETRIEVER MIX NAMED BOZLEY. I WOULD PASS WISDOM BY WHISPERING INTO HIS EAR AT TIMES. I THINK THIS HELPED BOZLEY GUIDE HIS FAMILY. IN SEPTEMBER OF 2020, BOZLEY PASSED OVER TO THE RAINBOW BRIDGE. BEFORE HE LEFT, HE WHISPERED INTO THE EAR OF THEIR NEW PUPPY LUNA, THE THINGS SHE NEEDED TO KNOW ABOUT HER FAMILY. THUS, CONTINUING THE TRADITION OF PASSING WISDOM ON, AS I HAD DONE YEARS BEFORE.

LINDA FINISHED THIS BOOK IN 2020 WHILE LIVING WITH A DEAR FRIEND MARYJO. IT WAS A DREAM COME TRUE FOR SHE LIVED NEAR LAKE SUPERIOR. FOR SEVEN MONTHS, LINDA WOULD WALK TO BRIGHTON BEACH. OFTENTIMES WHILE SITTING AT THE GAZEBO, SHE WOULD FEEL MY SPIRIT CLOSE TO HER. THE CIRCLE OF OUR LIVES WOULD ALWAYS REMAIN CONNECTED.   ~ CORKY

CORKY THE WONDERDOG SONG...

Linda and her friend Glenda composed this song about me, Kieran, and Reeve added the last verse for all to enjoy!!

Corky the Wonderdog You were a friend to me Corky the Wonderdog You taught me to be free.

Corky the Wonderdog

You filled our hearts with glee Corky the Wonderdog.

Thank you for coming to me.

Corky the Wonderdog

You loved to play and run Filling our lives with much joy and cheering us up with fun.

Corky the Wonderdog

You taught us to rise up for what's right Corky the Wonderdog.

We love you with all of our might.

Kieran and Reeve's verse!

Corky the Wonderdog

You were such a good dog Corky the Wonderdog.

You ate just like a hog!!!